D1086608

100 Smokin' Hot Cannabis Marketing Hacks

(Out-of-the-box marketing hacks for cannabis, CBD and hemp)

Darrell Griffin, MBA, CPA

By Darrell Griffin CPA, MBA

100 Smokin' Hot Cannabis Marketing Hacks

Copyright © 2021 by Darrell Griffin and Easy Brain Labs, Inc.

All rights reserved. No part of this publication may be reproduced, distributed, or transmitted in any form or by any means, including photocopying, recording, or other electronic or mechanical methods, without the prior written permission of the publisher, except in the case of brief quotations embodied in critical reviews and certain other noncommercial uses permitted by copyright law. For permission requests, write to the publisher, addressed "Attention: Permissions Coordinator," at the address below.

Easy Brain Labs, Inc.

www.easybrainlabs.com

ISBN: 978-1-68524-554-2

Ordering Information:
Quantity sales. Special discounts are available on quantity purchases by corporations, associations, and others. For details, contact the publisher at the address above.
Orders by U.S. trade bookstores and wholesalers. Please contact Easy Brain Labs Distribution: visit www.easybrainlabs.com.

Contents

Disclaimer:

Although the author and publisher have made every effort to ensure that the information in this book was correct at press time, the author and publisher do not assume and hereby disclaim any liability to any party for any loss, damage, or disruption caused by errors or omissions, whether such errors or omissions result from negligence, accident, and/ or other cause.

The author and publisher do not render legal or accounting advice. Please consult your legal counsel and/or accountant to properly determine the legal and accounting implications of any of the information included in this book.

I dedicate this book to my family

I dedicate this book to my wife, Kim. She has been my rock for over 37 years and has always encouraged my writing. And to my two youngest children, Alexis and Jordan, who had to endure my late blooming desires to put my thoughts on paper. All 3 were lovingly accommodating to my frequent moodiness, late night hours, and the smell of cannabis growing in my office.

Acknowledgements

Jesus and God for loaning me the tools of life while I briefly visit this planet.

Kim – My wife, my biggest critic, and my biggest fan. I wish I could do half of what she thinks I can do.

Alexis – My daughter, who once left a note on my desk that said, "Better to write for yourself and have no public, than to write for the public and have no self." – Cyril Connolly.

Jordan – My son, who continuously teaches me that we are all the same on the inside and that autism is not less, it is just different. He has earned a black belt in Tae Kwon Do and is well on his way to finishing his college degree with honors.

Craig Duswalt – A master marketer, entrepreneur, mentor, creative thinker. Craig helped me learn to color outside the lines in business. This book is a result of Craig's coloring lessons.

Phyllis Duarte and Alexis Griffin – My editors who add coherence to my ramblings.

Richard Barchard – My cousin and the first smoking partner I can remember.

Pastor Rick Kasel and his prayer warrior wife Jane – Rick, you have been one of my best friends. There are very few people that know they Bible better than you and Jane. Conservatives that do not embrace the cannabis lifestyle but they still include me among their friends.

Sheila, Sharon, and Sandra – My sisters who have always been inspirations to say what was on my mind.

Vance Paulson – My high school counselor that told me **never** to go to college. I ignored his advice and went on to college, graduating with a perfect 4.00 GPA with an MBA from California State University, Stanislaus.

Pastor Dudley Rutherford – Pastor at Shepherd Church who always says it like it is. A Bible based preacher at the world famous Shepherd Church in Porter Ranch, CA. He is conservative and I aspire to live my faith 24/7 the way he does.

SSG. Darrell Ray Griffin, Jr. (KIA, Baghdad, Iraq, March 21, 2007) – My son, who shared my love of the written word, of family, and of Country.

Chris Marston – CEO of Exemplar Business, who gave me the opportunity to get more immersed in cannabis consulting.

Phil Margo – My dear friend and the singer from the Tokens that made the song, "The Lion sleeps tonight" world famous over 50 years ago. Phil has always helped me see things from a different perspective with a healthy dose of liberal thought.

Guillermo Salazar – My wife's cousin's husband. An incredible artist and liberal thought provocateur who has made me think about complex things simply and simple things complexly.

James Woods – Actor, intellect, and man of independent thought. I have watched you defy your industry, tossing caution to the wind. When you put your thoughts out there, you will not always be popular but you will be honest with yourself.

Out of the Shadows and Under the Magnifying Glass

. You have waited years for the moment you could come out of the shadows and LEGALLY sell CANNABIS, one of the most important plants that God has given to us. Now let's sell some cannabis. The cannabis industry is the fastest growing industry on the planet; the government, the people, and the churches are looking at the cannabis industry anew. This brings a certain amount of unwanted regulation, curiosity, and scrutiny. There are many big companies and small operators who want to build their cannabis companies now, but how? Certainly not by doing the same tired marketing all the other cannabis companies are doing. Be different. Get noticed. A good start is reading ***100 Smokin' Hot Cannabis Marketing Hacks.***

Billie Eilish sings in one of her songs, "My boy's an ugly crier, but he's such a pretty liar." Don't be that guy. Keep it positive. Keep it real.

A Short Overview of the Basic Principles of Marketing

We are assuming that you are doing all of the basics in marketing such as an e-commerce enabled website, SEO, social media postings, and all the other advertising "tricks" used by your competition. "100 Smokin' Hot" ideas is about doing things your competition is not.

You really need to know about the basics to fully appreciate and effectively implement "100 Smokin' Hot Marketing Hacks." Combine them and you are on your way to running a successful cannabis company.

Marketing Mix

Product/ Service	Price	Promotion	Place	People
Functionality	Selling Price	Sponsorships	Distribution Channels	Services Provided
Appearance/ Product Attributes	Discounts	Advertising	Logistics	Attitude
Warranty	Payment Arrangements	Public Relations Activities	Service Levels	Customer Service
Quality	Price Matching Services	Message	Location	Appearance
Packaging	Credit Terms	Media	Marketing Coverage	Employee Portrayal

A "P" I will add that is not part of the standard marketing mix is "Planning." Too often cannabis companies leave marketing to chance, but planning is a critical component to success. You need a detailed marketing plan. Failing to plan is planning to fail.

Let's touch on each one of these.

Product/ Service

Your product and/or service is why you are in business. You are probably selling cannabis, or something related to cannabis if you bought this book.

Functionality

Looking pretty and appealing is important but if your product does not work as advertised then it will not sell. People buy cannabis to feel better physically and/or mentally. If your product does not deliver as advertised, as it appears in pictures, and at the potency listed on the label, your product will not sell.

Here is where the slogan, "Under promise and over deliver" is really important. I recently tried a new crumble by Just Cannabis called "Sugar." The packaging is simple elegance. When you remove the lid from the jar, your nose gets a hint of the sweetness you are about to enjoy. The rich root beer-colored granules fall easily off your dabbing tool. The smoking experience is smooth and sweet as is the fragrance.

The name of this incredible product is "Sugar." Supremely understated.

Picture provided courtesy of Superior Herbal Health

Picture provided courtesy of Superior Herbal Health

Superior Herbal Health has incredible packaging. Their website has much more than just a description with the product; they paint a whole experience.

Our THC crystals are formed from the extract of the finest cannabis strains while the original terpene

sauce is locked into the thc crystalline structure preserving the incredible flavor of the flower. Our THCa "Sugar" is a full spectrum cannabis extract. Potent and delicious, Just Cannabis "Sugar" is best experienced through low temperature dabbing."

With this packaging and this product experience description, of course, this product is super successful. The great thing about legal cannabis is the extensiveness of the required labeling. I recently bought an eighth from a local dispensary. Here is the information included on the jar:

Sativa
Total Cannabinoids – 23.32%
Batch - #x-xx-xxxx

Given the lab certification requirements you have some level of assurance that the cannabis that you buy will perform as indicated.

Strain: Strawberry Fields
THCa/g: 220.47 mg
CBDa/g: 0.34 mg
Packaged on :12.18.19
Cultivated by AAA- XX-XXXXXXX

Contact@XXXXXX.com

WWW.XXXXXXX.com

Appearance/ Product Attributes

If cannabis doesn't look good sitting in the sampler unit or it does not look good when the budtender brings it to the counter, it will end up not selling. Just like people thump and smell their watermelons or sniff their oregano, they smell their cannabis when they are about to purchase. Your products have to taste good, smell good, and look good at the dispensary and when your customers get them home.

Warranty

People want to have some assurances that they are getting what they pay for. They expect you to warrant that the products they are selling will perform as advertised. The brands that you carry must stand behind their products. Their advertising should promote their high level of quality,

Quality

Inferior products will generate inferior sales or no sales. Quality has to be consistent. Quality has to permeate your product. A great product in crappy packaging is still a crappy product. Cannabis quality is not all about appearance. It has to smell good. It has to be the potency listed. It has to taste good. It has to look good. It has to be good and it has to be good consistently.

Packaging

There is a multitude of buyer options for all product lines of cannabis. Why will people buy your products or go to your cannabis store instead of the competitors? If you are a retail shop, maybe you have the best selection of shatter, or you sell only sun-grown flower. Quality is important, but your customers have to pick up your product to judge its quality. Packaging is critically important when selling cannabis products. Normally, I would say take the subtle, classy approach to packaging cannabis.

But sometimes you just have to be in your customer's face. Take Zax-Wax as an example.

Zax-Wax has achieved almost cult status by being "out-there." Having uncompromising quality concentrate (incredible crumble) and rising above the cannabis marketing clutter. I personally feel that Zax-Wax has some of the best crumble available and they are not shy about telling how good their products are.

Price

Are you trying to be the best priced prerolls? Are you priced to compete with other middle shelf edibles? Or, are you a top shelf, sun grown, organic, intense strain, in demand product? It is always easier to go down in price than it is to go up in price. Cannabis is a product that cries premium. Quality matters and quality costs more. You do get what you pay for!

Pricing your products is an art, not a science. The most common price strategies are Premium Pricing, Value Pricing, Cost-Plus Pricing, Competitive Pricing, Penetration Pricing, and Skimming. Your pricing strategies should not be handcuffs but will be your overall approach to maximization of profits for your company.

Premium Pricing

Is there something unique about you product? It is a little hard to premium price your flower when there are 6 other flowers in the case with the same potency, strain and all are priced 5 dollars below your flower.

If you are a premium priced cannabis product and you find some other brand trying to enter your market, your first knee-jerk reaction is to drop your price. Normally a bad move. No one wins in a price war. Consider one or more of these maneuvers:

1.Keep your price the same but consider a discount based on loyalty or some other special factor.

2.Introduce a sub-premium version of your product that will help you capture the value shoppers, while keeping your premium product-pricing model intact.

Value Pricing

Value-based pricing is pricing based on the customers perceived benefits of the products instead of on the exact costs of developing the product. Some good examples of these types of products are art, fashion and, of course, cannabis. The value you pay for a painting is not based on the costs of the brushes, paints, and canvas. Prada does not command top dollar in the fashion industry based on the fabrics it uses. Its high prices are based on its perceived value.

There are value-based products in the cannabis marketplace. A great example is *Leafs By Snoop (LBS)*.

According to company literature, Snoop Dogg was directly involved in the selection of every single product offered by LBS. The bottom line is, if Snoop is involved, the cannabis has to be good.

Cost-Plus Pricing

This is probably the most widely used pricing in most industries, including the cannabis industry. This pricing method basically takes your purchase price and multiplies it by a markup factor.

The formula for calculating cost plus is as follows:

Retail = Cost + (markup percentage x cost)

If you pay $10 for an eighth and want to mark it up 250% multiply $10 by 250% (200% + 50%) and your price will be $25.

Competitive Pricing

Here you are trying to keep your pricing at parity with your primary competitors. This is a little dangerous because you don't really know what your competitors cost structures are. You don't know any of their various costs such as marketing and personnel. This is kind of like flying by instruments.

There are a lot of non-product considerations:

- Shorter lines
- Home delivery
- Product assembly
- Speed of service

- Satisfactory handling of customer complaints
- "No questions asked" return policy
- Employees knowledge of product and/or service
- Friendly employees
- Convenient or exclusive location
- Ease of ordering (e.g. "one button" ordering website, etc.)
- Free wrapping and mailing
- Free coffee and donuts
- Product training
- Easy payment plans

These are individual tools that you can use to be more competitive when your primary competitor(s) is playing the competitive pricing game.

Pricing Below the Competition

The strategy of pricing below the competition is not an effective long-term strategy. There will always be someone that can price below you and quickly take market share from you. Pricing below the competition will reduce your strategic options. Here are some points you will want to consider with pricing below the competition:

- Obtain the best possible prices for your merchandise
- Locate your business in an inexpensive location
- Closely monitor inventory
- Pay close attention to Economic Order Quantity calculations
- Limit your products to fast moving items. At low prices, you cannot afford to have them sitting on your shelves for an extended period of time
- Your advertising should concentrate on prices
- Limit your other services

Penetration Pricing

This type of pricing is a type of pricing below the competition. This is normally a short-term strategy aimed at quickly gaining market share. This strategy normally is combined with a strategy where you eventually raise your prices.

Skimming Pricing

When you introduce a product that everyone wants, you have the opportunity to take some extra profits. Remember when the fidget spinners hit the market? This little toy was going for $10 to

$20. The exact same toy was selling for $3 to $5 just 6 months later. Early adopters are normally willing to pay a premium to be one of the first to use a new product.

Price Lining

This is when a merchant targets a specific segment of consumers by carrying products only in a specified price rate. High-end sellers and low-end sellers use this strategy effectively. At the low end, the "98 Cent" stores in Southern California have successfully used price lining. They sell everything from dog food to auto accessories using price lining. You can go to Rodeo Drive in Beverly Hills and see high-end price lining at work in a number of clothing shops.

Promotion

This includes all of the activities that you employ to get customers to your stores or to buy your products. These activities include public relations, advertising, sponsorships and community events. You want to attract a clientele to your store that will be continuing customers. You don't want to do the old hard sales approach. Cannabis is still new as a retail product. Education and being subtle are the current keys to cannabis promotion. Having a doper with bloodshot eyes and a joint in his mouth is not subtle. Have the same guy, nicely dressed sitting in his Herman Miller office chair with a nice vape is more subtle. Education is important because cannabis has been in the shadows for decades and many people who are unfamiliar with its benefits or are simply misinformed are just now beginning to get curious about it and want to try it. We want to inform people of the benefits of cannabis but don't beat the consumers over the head with an aggressive ad talking about getting "F'd" up.

Place

This is where your customers meet your product. It may be at your store or it may be online. The easier it is for your customers to get your products, the more you will sell. With cannabis, there are a few more restrictions than your normal consumer products, so you must be more creative.

This part of the marketing equation covers getting your product in front of your customers so they can decide to buy your product. It is all about logistics, locations, and doing whatever it takes to get your products and services in front of your customers.

People

This is the magical part of the equation. This is your staff, salespeople, and everyone else within the company that helps get your products in the hands of your customers. Every single person at your company, whether it be the bookkeeper, the janitor, or the CFO, is capable of being a salesperson. You can't sell your cannabis out of a vending machine. You need people to be successful.

Cannabis Advertising Laws and Regulations

Each state that allows the sale of cannabis will have its own laws and regulations regarding the sale of cannabis. Be sure to consult with the cannabis regulatory agencies in your state about the specific laws for cannabis advertising.

According to a leading authority in the cannabis industry, "A retail marijuana store may not use giveaway coupons as promotional materials or conduct promotional activities such as games or competitions to encourage sale of marijuana or marijuana products."[1] Check with the regulatory agencies in your individual state.

---

[1] https://www.leafly.com/news/industry/state-by-state-guide-to-cannabis-advertising-regulations

Let's Look at Our 100 Smokin' Cannabis Marketing Hacks.

Products

1. Let Your Clients Pick Your Products

Have in store contests to allow your customers to select a "Specially Selected" section of your store, newsletter, or website. This works for all levels of the cannabis business. If you are a distributor, your retailers want to know what products are moving; those "specially selected" products.

2. Put Your Popular Products at the Back of the Store

Grocery stores are smart about where they put their popular products. Have you ever noticed that milk and produce are always at the back of the store? Grocers know that you will pick up other items for purchase as you travel to the back of their stores to grab your milk and eggs. Do the same at your dispensaries. Put your popular bud at the back of the store with all kinds of purchase opportunities between the bud and the front door.

3. Be Touched By Your Clients

Have empty samples of your products, clearly marked EMPTY SAMPLE so your clients can get an idea of the feel, weight and look of the product they are thinking about purchasing. I have bought more than one disposable vape cartridge that has a tip I did not like. I would not have made this mistake had I been able to examine it before purchasing it.

Price

4. Price High When Your Competition Prices Low

When the big guy prices his top shelf bud at $40 and you are pricing yours at $55, his bud will sell more than your bud. $15 is a substantial price difference. If you have similar bud as far as the look, feel, smell, and potency, then you should do something different to justify that price for the customer. Perhaps something along the lines of giving a digital book away with the product. Something that is little additional cost; high perceived value.

5. Selling Systems

Infomercials have been successful in part because the products they are selling are demonstrable. People love demonstrations and they love systems, outfits, and tool sets. This is why upsells and cross sales work. If I buy the food dehydrator, I have to buy the extra trays that are offered on the same commercial at a deep discount. When fidget spinners were successful people had to have spinner displays. People that like to work on cars love to have big toolboxes. If you have a product that may be a little high priced for its category make it part of a system, part of a set. Give a free plastic rolling tray with your premium bud. Offer a free carb cap with your premium shatter.

Promotion

6. Host Free Events

Reporters are always looking for a good story. Give them what they want and get some free publicity by hosting a free event. You will get more response if there's food or freebies involved. Use this list of 109 ways to get media attention https://copyblogger.com/irresistible-pr/ to make the most of any event.

7. Use Voice Mail and Autoresponder

Most states restrict the hours cannabis shops can be open. You can use voice mail programs and autoresponders to let your customers know about your special offers. It's a great way to get your message across during closed hours. It will not cost you a penny!

8. Join Associations and Use the Provided Resources

Join associations and encourage your staff to get involved. These opportunities include local networking events, online forums, and job boards. The more people you know, the more customers you will have.

9. Enter Business Award Competitions

If you win, you get a badge on your website and a lot more sales. Even if you do not win, you can still get a lot of publicity if you place high enough and broadcast your participation.

10. Write Articles for AARP or AMAC

The baby boomers are the biggest growing consumer segment for cannabis. All of the old hippies (there is a little hippie in anyone over the age of fifty) are enjoying being able to integrate cannabis into their lifestyles.

11. Frequent Buyer Plan

Loyalty programs work because of what's known as the "Pareto Principle"—aka the 80/20 rule. It says that 20% of your customers account for 80% of revenue and acquiring a new customer can cost as much as 7X more than retaining an existing one[2].

You need to have a frequent buyer plan. Reward that cannabis buyer that comes in every week. The average amount spent for

---

[2] https://flowhub.com/learn/blog/cannabis-loyalty-programs-reward-repeat-dispensary-customers

cannabis, per visit is between $60 and $80.[3] The average recreational user purchases every 13.69 days and every medical user purchases every 10.25 days.[4] You want both of these types of consumers coming into your store as "their" store. Establish a program where every time your customer makes a purchase of anything from your store, they gets frequent buyer credits.

This same loyal customer should be on your weekly newsletter. There should be deals in the store and online offered only to loyal buyers and customers on the subscription list. These customers are going to buy somewhere, make sure it is at your store. Do not just put together your frequent buyer plan like all the other cannabis dispensaries. Do not be boring.

There are 6 elements to a good customer loyalty plan[5]

- A great loyalty plan is frictionless. Joining and using a loyalty program should be easy.
- Make your loyalty rewards exclusive. Don't fear exclusivity. If something is available to everyone, it can seem less valuable.
- Make your loyalty campaign repeatable. The difference between an offer and a loyalty

---

[3] https://mjbizdaily.com/chart-week-average-marijuana-dispensary-purchase-amounts-range-60-100/

[4] https://www.statista.com/statistics/795108/purchase-frequency-of-cannabis-in-north-america-by-market/

[5] https://www.womply.com/blog/the-6-elements-of-an-effective-loyalty-program/

program is an offer is normally available at time of purchase and is a “one off.”

- A loyalty program normally accumulates encouraging repeated purchases.
- A good loyalty program compels action from customers. The loyalty program should encourage purchasing again and again.
- Make sure your loyalty plan is “on brand.”

Most successful brands use customer loyalty programs because they work.

- Sephora Beauty Insider – 17 million loyal members, makes up 80% of Sephora’s sales[6].
- Starbucks Rewards – Their points expire creating a sense of urgency. I always make sure I use my points before they expire.
- Amazon Prime – Prime members spend an average of 4 times more than other Amazon customers.
- TOMS - Does not give customers a loyalty card or offer rewards for every purchase. Instead, they appeal to their customers’ values and sense of worth. With every purchase, customers earn the non-monetary

[6] https://www.shopify.com/blog/loyalty-program

incentive of creating change through various initiatives like the One for One shoe donation.

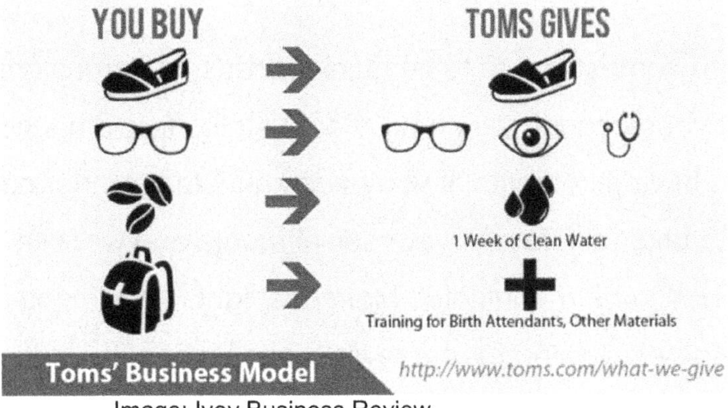

Image: Ivey Business Review

Here are some ideas that will work specifically in a cannabis store:

- Bring a friend reward. How cool is this? You get your regular customer in and you get a potential new customer to come into your store. Your biggest advocate is your customer.
- Give cool rewards. Nowadays, it is all about safety. Come in frequently and get a box of free masks. Or maybe really cool designer masks. You can probably get one or more of your vendors to supply the masks for free if they are able to include their logos on the masks. In this current environment, custom-made masks are inexpensive and could be an added incentive for

spending a certain dollar amount and will be cheap advertising.

12. **Instant In-store Contests**

In store contests have to be quick because your customers are not at your location very long. Some states forbid cannabis stores having contests. If you have an instant winner contest, be sure to take pictures for your social media and website. The prize has to be meaningful. Make the lights go off, ring a bell, and stop everything for the few seconds when the instant winner is identified. This will be great for the lucky customer and an incentive for the other customers in the store. This will also be newsletter worthy.

13. **Surprise! We All Like Surprises**

Photo by Getty Images

Once or twice a day, randomly pay for one of your customer's purchase. This is a strategy that needs to be promoted to be effective. Once you begin these promotions you must get the word out. Imagine what your customers and potential customers will do when they read, "Do you feel lucky today? XX lucky customers will get their purchase today paid for in full.

14. Do Not Aim Your Marketing at the Pot Heads

They will buy what they want even if your store looks like a portable toilet. They are probably growing their own anyway. The smart idea would be to market to the sustainable clients with jobs that want a nice comfortable shopping experience. There are more millennials than baby boomers, but the average baby boomer has 8X the personal wealth of the average millennial. Make sure your marketing and store reflect what your customers strive to be, how they perceive themselves[7].

15. Celebrity Faces or Events on Mugs

---

[7] https://www.lexingtonlaw.com/blog/credit-cards/baby-boomer-spending-habits.html

Photo by Getty Images

Agree to put a celebrity face on your cannabis packages in exchange for shout outs. This is a symbiotic relationship. The celebrity gets publicity and so do you. For your local dispensary, put a local celebrity, local events, and local happenings on one of your labels.

Some sample ideas:

- "Thank you, grocery checks union #XX,"
- "Thank you, Devonshire Division Police Department,"
- "Quarantine is over, let's get social"
- "Farmers market every Tuesday"
- "Thank you to our returning soldier Joseph White"

16. Free Cup of Coffee, Keep the Mug

Photo by Getty Images

Everyone loves mugs. Especially the free ones and the free ones with Starbucks gift certificates are even better. That mug may end up sitting on someone's desk at the office screaming at your customer's office mates. Have a free mug day. The first 100 people to come in today get a free mug.

17. Trade Advertising with Local Businesses and Organizations

There are direct and indirect benefits from trading advertising with local businesses. You are advertising to your partnering company's customers and, in a way, the partnering company is endorsing you. This will also help you blend into your community. Trade advertising with local gyms, drinking establishments, sandwich shops, convenience stores, tire shops.

What goes better with a good blunt than a burrito?

18. Put Other Regular People's Faces on Your Jars and Packaging

Photo by Easy Brain Labs

This can be approached in several different ways. You can make it a money maker where people pay to have their friends, families, and associate's pictures on your packaging, or select products, displays, website, etc. for special events in their lives. Another option is to select random customers and feature them on your products for a month. This is, of course, after asking for their permission.

19. Commemorate Events

Cannabis companies have only recently been able to come out of the shadows. Now we can live in the light and openly contribute to our communities. It is important to create as many impressions with your customers and potential customers as possible. Why not create some of these impressions by helping the community? It would make sense for a dispensary to team up with the local Red Cross to promote a safety program or host local fundraising events.

20. Fix the Tiny Bag/Empty Big Bag Issue

Give a bigger bag and stuff it with freebies and informational literature. Your customer bags are a valuable resource. There are advertising opportunities in the bag and on the outside of the bag as well. I love to open my dispensary bag and have all kinds of free stuff fall out as long as it is not junk. Bling bags have always been popular in Hollywood at all the self-indulgent award shows.

A lot of stores sell placement real estate in their stores in the way of end caps and favorably placed shelves. You can sell the real estate on the inside and outside of your bags. You can get your vendors to pay for placement on your bags.

Lawyers will probably be the first to advertise on cannabis product bags, but most local businesses that do not involve kids are advertising candidates.

21. Don't Buy Your Own Bags

Let a brand buy your customer bags for free advertising on the bags, which can be inserted with your brochures or bag samples.

Think of the free things that can go into your customer bags that you can probably get for free:

1. Lighters
2. Rolling trays
3. Carb caps
4. Rolling papers
5. One hitters
6. Crumble keepers
7. Dosing guides
8. Single joint containers
9. Key chains
10. Sample bong cleaners

22. Advertise on Shopping Bags

Pay for shopping bags at local bars and liquor stores with your brand and/or dispensary name on their bags. Some places that might take your subtle advertising bags:

1.Bars

2.Incense/ candle shops

3. Liquor stores

4.Private gyms

5.Head shops

6.Popup restaurants

7. Swap meets

8. Used/ new bookstores

9. Health food stores

23. Yoga studios

We are not just talking about your everyday brown paper bags. For a yoga studio, they might be pleased if you supplied them with cheap drawstring bags displaying their logo and your subtle logo.

24. Start Selling in the Lobby

This idea has to be tempered with depending on how much exposure your lobby has to the street and how your state regulates lobby advertising. You only have a few minutes to sell to your customers so start the sales process as soon as possible. When they walk in the door, hand them sales literature, or the freebie for the day. You need big flat screen monitors in your lobby getting your clients ready for the sales adventure once they enter the selling floor. Engage your customers as early in the engagement process as possible.

25. Cleanup the Neighborhood

Photo by Getty Images

Organize a neighborhood weed-pulling event to spruce up the neighborhood. Some weeds are good but some weeds are not. Of course, make sure you get press coverage for this. If you work in conjunction with your neighborhood council, you can get some free publicity in their public newsletter. You might want to consider giving your staff time off to volunteer. Imagine the excellent public relations created for your dispensary when it becomes known in your neighborhood as the Weed Patrol: keeping the wrong kind of weeds out of your neighborhood.

26. Keep Your Highways Litter Free

You have seen the signs along the freeway that shows civil minded companies that donate to keeping our country looking good. Organize a freeway clean up. The name of your company will be posted on the section of the freeway; you keep the freeway litter free, and will also serve as free advertising that is visible to a large number of people.

Photo provided by Easy Brain Labs, Inc.

These can be great devices for leaving impressions on your potential customers minds. If you are like most people, your eyes are drawn to these signs in part because there is very little ad competition along the sides of freeways. These signs will typically cost you from $100 to $350 a sign per month.

27. Everyone Loves Tee shirts

Photo provided by Getty Images

Tee shirts are America's contribution to fashion. We all love tee shirts. The first thing we like to do when we get off the plane at our vacation destination is buy a tee shirt. Tee shirts are great, cheap, and effective walking billboards. Here are some ideas for adding tee shirts into your marketing mix:

1. Give away randomly with purchases
2. Occasionally during the day stop everything and throw out some tee shirts
3. Have an old-fashioned tie dye tee shirt contest
4. Have a tie dye tee shirt day where you give a discount for everyone who wears a tie dye tee shirt
5. Have a tee shirt design contest

6. Always have a trunk full of tee shirts when you speak at any function

People will instantly love you as a speaker if you start off your presentation by throwing out some tee shirts. I was at Craig DeWalt's "Rockstar Marketing Bootcamp" when he came on stage and started shooting tee shirts out of a cannon. The audience went crazy. Dignified executives in Brooks Brother suits jumped to their feet blocking their fellow seminar attendees to grab one of the flying tee shirts. Tee shirts are walking billboards, so make them as cool as possible. Don't cheap out. This may be the only image your potential clients have of your establishment. Give them away with purchases, when you speak at functions, and when you send samples to potential client dispensaries. I saw a great line on a tee shirt the other day, "Cannabis is much more dignified than weed."

Tee shirts are a way of putting hundreds of billboards on the street.

28. Hold Cannabis Cooking Classes

Everyone loves to cook. A lot of people are curious about cooking with cannabis. These classes can be such customer magnets that if you don't have a room at your dispensary, grow location, or manufacturing facility for classes, you should consider renting a small lecture room somewhere to give weekly or monthly classes. Start with the basics on how to make cannabutter and cannaoil. Extend your cooking classroom onto your website and email newsletters.

29. Names are Soooo Important

Always, always refer to your customers by their names. Make them feel that they are special because they are special. Without them, you will not be in business very long. Instead of “Next guest please,” it sounds so much better to say , “You are next Cheech,” of course, if your name is Cheech. It makes no sense not to do this. You already have the customer’s name when their identifications are verified before entering your store.

30. Don’t Call Me Sir - Respect

We all like to be perceived as how we want to be, not how we necessarily are at the moment. I am older and I hate it when people refer to me as Mr. Griffin. I always think, “That’s my Dad,” when people refer to me as “Sir.” Yes, I want respect but do not make me feel old. The same holds true for the millennials that walk into your shops. Respect them. Do not refer to them as “Kid.”

31. Hold Cannabis Informational Seminars

Knowledge is power. Trite, but true. We live in an information driven world. Here are a few topics to get you started:

1.Ways to use cannabis

2.Exercise and cannabis

3.Cooking with cannabis

4. The plant

5. Health and cannabis

6.DIY classes

7. Seniors and cannabis

8. The science of cannabis

32. Speak on the Radio

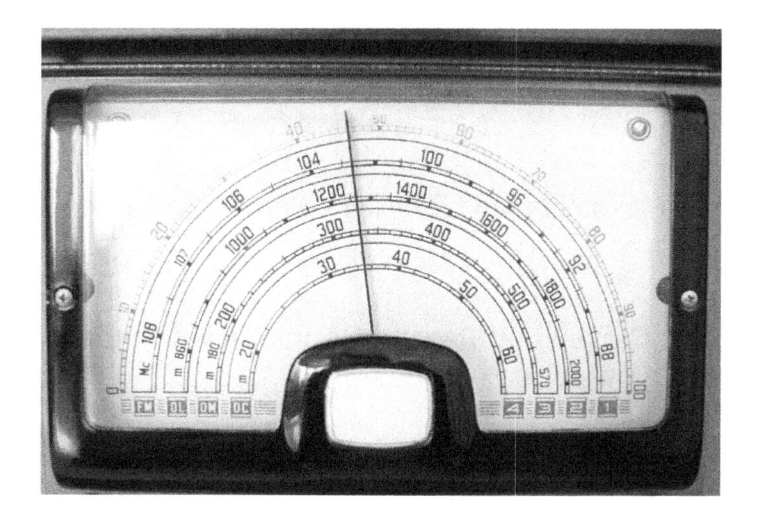

Photo provided by Getty Images

Radio reaches about 90% of all U.S. adults. There are over 15,500 (terrestrial) radio stations in the U.S.. We now have terrestrial and internet radio stations. The number of internet radio stations is rapidly growing. It looks like more and more people are going to join the streaming audio bandwagon. According to Rain News, audio streaming listening hours are estimated to grow more than 40 percent, from 30 billion in 2014 to 43 billion in 2017. That plays out to be roughly 180 million U.S. digital radio listeners, per eMarketer. It's no wonder, considering streaming radio is pretty good at what it does.[8] Two-thirds of 18 – 34-year-olds listen to online radio monthly.

There are a lot fewer restrictions on internet radio stations. Internet radio involves streaming media, presenting listeners with a continuous stream of audio that typically cannot be paused or replayed, much like traditional broadcast media; in this respect, it is distinct from on-demand file serving. Internet radio is also distinct from podcasting, which involves downloading rather than streaming.

There are an estimated 52 million internet radio listeners. There are a number of internet radio directories available online.

33. Have Classes on Pairing Cannabis with the Right Foods, Places, and Movies

[8] https://www.edgewatergoldradio.com/blank-1/2018/08/30/Internet-Radio-vs-Terrestrial-Radio#!, Jim Murphy, August 30, 2020

Photo provided by Getty Images

Cannabis is more than a plant, more than a medicine, more than a social lubricant. It is an integral part of today's progressive life style. It adds balance to an otherwise overly crazy lifestyle. Here are some ideas of what you can pair with cannabis:

1. Wines
2. Beers
3. Desserts
4. Main course
5. Music
6. Movies
7. Holidays
8. Regions – Every region has its local favorite. Puff yours, puff theirs.
9. Exercises

10. Sporting events
11. Soups
12. Art
13. Events
14. Teas/ coffees
15. Candies/ chocolates
16. Fruits/ vegetables
17. Herbs and spices
18. Hard liquor pairings (e.g., vodka, gin, tequila, etc.)
19. Board game parings
20. Video game pairings
21. Book genres
22. Meats

34. White Coats Speak Volumes

Have a doctor come in and give a presentation on the medical benefits of cannabis (THC and CBD). Everyone knows doctors always tell the truth.

35. Don't Keep Secrets – Do Press Releases

Do press releases every time, any time anything newsworthy happens. Marketing is about making impressions, about filling a want or a need. Potential clients/patients need to be familiar with the name of your dispensary. Press releases are more believable than straight advertising. There are other benefits also. If you do a broadcast with one of the PR wire services you will have airtime or press coverage on major media outlets like Fox. Then you can add “As seen on Fox TV” on your website.

36. Sponsor/Volunteer for a Charity

There is an endless list of worthy causes. Besides, God has blessed you with a great cannabis business so you should do something to give back. A quick example is the Multiple Sclerosis Foundation.

They have lots of opportunities to get involved, really involved. You can sponsor an event, sponsor tee shirts, and get involved.

37. Sponsor a Good Old Fashion Rock Concert

Imagine seeing your logo on the backs of 10,000 screaming fans. Consider small venues that have less than a thousand fans. They go begging for sponsors. Can't afford to be a tee shirt sponsor? Then be a program sponsor.

38. Join Chamber of Commerce

A lot of legitimate companies join their local credit unions but I bet there will not be very many cannabis shops in the Chamber of Commerce. You can probably have your local chamber to yourself. It's a great way to get your name out there in the community. It instantly makes your clinic friendlier to the community. How cool is a Chamber of Commerce sticker in your front window?

39. Swag Bags

A cannabis company contributed a brochure to the swag bag that Chicago Marathon runners received last fall. The brochure entitled "Welcome to a State of Relief" provided information about the Illinois medical marijuana program. The document had to pass muster with race sponsor Bank of America. "It had to be elevated all the way up to corporate in New York," said Charles Bachtell, founder and CEO of Cresco Labs. Cannabis and cannabis related products are ideal items for a swag bag. As the name implies, do not put your rejects in the swag bags.[9]Another cannabis company sponsored professional skier Tanner Hall, an X Games gold medalist. Together, Hall and the company developed the Tanner Hall Skiboss Collection featuring

---

[9] https://mjbizmagazine.com/4-novel-marijuana-marketing-strategies/

"everything you need to roll a joint on the go," including papers, a grinder and a lighter. The accessories can be carried in Black Rock's flagship "stash box." https://mjbizmagazine.com/4-novel-marijuana-marketing-strategies.

40. Puff, Sip, & Paint Session

Have a painting training session yourself or supply the bud to a group doing it all already. Put a different spin on it and host a baking training class, a writing class, or a basket weaving class. They all are good marketing opportunities.

Place

41. Creating Chalk Art in Sidewalks

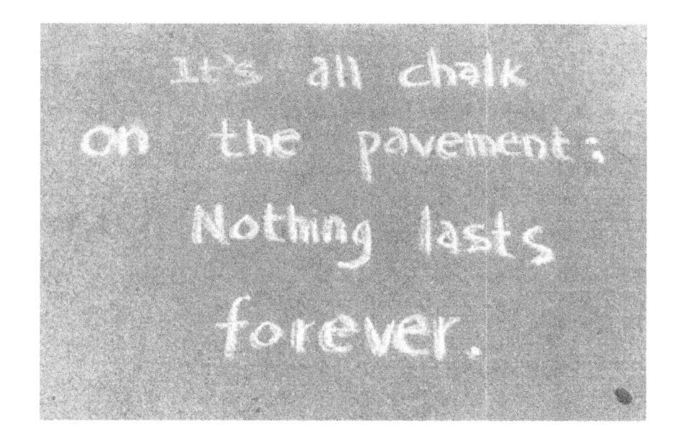

Photo provided by Easy Brain Labs, Inc.

Have one of your talented budtenders or a local artist create chalk drawings on the sidewalk out in front of your store. Maybe the side of your store, or in the store.

42. Happy Birthday Wall

After identifying that it is a particular client's birthday, text him and let him know that if he comes in today, he will get a birthday surprise. If he shows up on his birthday, his purchase is free, up to $50, and his picture is included on the birthday wall poster. Have him sign it like a rockstar. This has to be real. If you try faking this one with phony enthusiasm it will backfire in your face.

43. Let Local Talent Perform in Your Lobby

This is one of my favorite promotion ideas. No cost to you; exposure for the performer. Clowns, magicians, folk singers, jugglers, comedians, artists and chalk drawers.

44. Community Event Bulletin Board

Community bulletin boards have always been a useful tool, even before the advent of the computer. When I was a kid, I remember the hundreds of business cards at the neighborhood SaveMart. There would be business cards, notices for lost dogs, advertising circulars for local barbershops and auto repair shops. Consider putting up a bulletin board in your lobby and on your website. Make it look like an old-fashioned community bulletin board and allow your clients to post on it.

45. Expand the Walls of Your Dispensary

When your budtenders and drivers are out in the community, they are walking marketing opportunities. Do not be stingy on the tee shirts. Give every one of your staff members your logo merchandise. Give your budtenders business cards and encourage them to hand them out. Tell them never to hand out just one card but at least two when someone asks for them.

Make sure your delivery drivers are wearing your logo hats/tee shirts while they deliver your merchandise in your log bags.

Let your customers steal your pens and pencils. The name of the game is having your logo everywhere you can in the community.

46. Customers Love End Caps and Special Displays

Work a deal out with the cannabis store manager or general manager to get special placement of your cannabis product in their store. If you feel you can sell an additional 500 units of your bud at the dispensary in question and you have a price structure like the one below consider offering the general manager $500 for a month of preferential store placement. You will have generated an additional gross margin of $13,250:

Selling Price	$45.00	$30.00	$15.00
Gross Margin	$22.50	$15.00	$ 7.50

$22.50 x 500 = $112,500

You can differentiate by selling organic bud and thus sell them at a premium.

47. A Cup of Coffee Makes the Waiting Seem Shorter

If you have customer-waiting lines, set out a coffee pot in the morning and after lunch and/or keep a big icy bucket of sodas or other drinks in your lobby. You want your customers to enter your selling room as fresh as possible.

48. The Whole Cannabis Buying Experience

Cannabis is expensive. Buying it should be an experience. Does your dispensary look like a CVS or a Sephora? When you walk out of a cannabis store, you are normally walking out with a tiny little shopping bag. If you upgrade your store, you can upgrade your clients and increase the average order amount.
Setting up a cannabis store can be expensive. Building out a nice experience for your customers can be prohibitively expensive. Leasehold improvements can be expensive. Sometimes shabby chic is the answer. Your décor does not have to be expensive to be impressive but make it a complete experience.

49. Hold an Open House

Remember the open houses you had in grammar school? They were always fun. Have an open house where you display your products and have budtenders available to answer questions. Set up stations in your dispensary where people can go to during the open house for specific questions to be answered. Give the attendees a brochure telling them what to expect at the open house. Have a couple of stations that are general overviews in nature and then a few specific subject stations such as dabbing or DIY.

50. Have Classy, Informative Signage

Photo provided by Superior Herbal Health

The "Clinik (www.theclinikla.com) has a nice simple, memorable logo.

Signage does not have to be fancy, but it is what people think of when they think of your establishment. It needs to look professional and can't and shouldn't be about getting high. Make sure your signage is compatible with the rest of your marketing areas.

51. Sponsor MONTHLY Toy and Food Drives for Children's Homes

Everyone does toy drives for children around the holidays. Do kids not need toys during the rest of the year? You can do something really good and get some good publicity for spreading holiday cheer all year long.

52. Urinal Billboards

I saw my first urinal billboard one night at a popular drinking establishment. I was standing there at the urinal reading the ads. There was a local bookstore that advertised on the billboard. I wrote down the phone number and visited the bookstore the next morning. These urinal billboards have become very sophisticated. Some of them are even heat activated.

53. Mobile Billboards

Photo provided by doitoutdoors.com

You have seen these mobile, truck mounted billboards around town. Eaze, the cannabis distribution platform, uses mobile advertising very effectively. Mobile ads can take your billboards to where your events and/or customers are to maximize exposure.[10]

54. Prerolls from a Vending Machines

http://grasshopperkiosks.com/

[10] https://doitoutdoors.com/resources/blog/mobile-billboards-drive-cannabis-advertising/

It's real! Grasshopper Kiosks and Green Box make digital vending machines for dispensaries that carry anything from pre-rolls to beverages. You can place your company in their hi-res video touchscreens, or even wrap the entire machine in branding. Now imagine all the other sponsor-friendly things inside dispensaries.

55. Maximize Your Selling Time

You have your customers waiting in line because you have the coolest dispensary in the city. Why would you line up your customers in your waiting area without interacting with them? You spent your marketing dollars to get them into your store. Engage them – sell them, inform them, be their dispensary. Here are some things to include in your lobby:

A. Literature from the brands you carry
B. Guides on cannabis consumption
C. Community calendar
D. Pictures and information about the budtenders on duty. This is important. Your budtenders can sell more if your customers feel they know the budtenders before going into the store.
E. Lifestyle props that support the theme of your store. I was recently in one dispensary that had a library sounding name. They had the most extensive "library" (books for sale of course) on cannabis in the progressive lifestyle that I have ever seen. Nowadays, most customers will sit

and fidget with their cell phones while they are in line. It is the typical thing to do when you are waiting for anything in line. Why not give them something else to do while they are in line? Maybe sample some non-cannabis-infused products. There is one smart fully integrated cannabis company in Chatsworth, CA, that always gives its clients non-THC/CBD taste test products while they are waiting. This waiting time is normally "dead" time. Utilize it.

People

56. Sharable Experiences

Create experiences that people remember and want to talk about. Cannabis businesses have an opportunity to leverage experience marketing by creating shareable moments for their customers. Jardin Premium Cannabis Dispensary did this by setting up a video booth that records a short animation of each customer and sends it as a GIF file to the person's email address. That way, even if the consumer doesn't buy, you'll offer a fun way to capture their email addresses, which you can use later for email marketing[11].

57. Survey Your Customers and Employees for Great Ideas

Talking to your customers is an easy way to get incredible out-of-the-box Marketing Hacks. Consider starting an old-fashioned suggestion box.

58. Ask Your Customers for Referrals

Beat your shyness. Simply ask - and you'll receive. Most people like to make referrals to people that have given them quality service. Ask, but also make sure you follow up with a thank you note for the referral and another note when the referral materializes into a client.

---

[11] https://cannabiz.media/5-proven-marijuana-marketing-and-advertising-ideas-that-work/, Susan Gunelius | Jan 25, 2018 |

59. Join "Help a Reporter Out"

HARO is a free way to get media coverage. Register as an expert source on HARO and whenever a journalist needs a quality source for an article you will get an email. Reply if interested and who knows, maybe it is time for your business to be featured in The New York Times.

60. Hire Those Baby Boomers

They are a third of your customers. They have years of experience. They have influence. 29%of Baby Boomers ages 65 to 72 were working or looking for work. (Source: Pew Research Center)

61. Stress Fitness

According to Greenentrepreneur.com, 28%of those (cannabis users) in America who use cannabis work out an average of two times a week while 22% of non-users reported doing so. 36% of users reported working out three to five times a week in America compared to 34% of non-users.[12] Be subtle about it. Maybe have a rack of sports tee shirts, sweat bands, or sports posters in your store.

---

[12] https://www.greenentrepreneur.com/article/293097, Survey Finds Cannabis Users Are Educated, Fit, Sociable and Surprisingly Republican

62. Upsell, Cross-sell, Down-sell, Sell More

Always encourage budtenders to sell additional products. Just like any business that carries a primary product, the average sell can be increased by 20% just by having add-on products that budtenders know how to sell. Your budtenders must be professionally trained in personal selling techniques. They should be upselling to a bigger size or to a premium product. Cross-sell a battery to go with that vape cartridge your budtender just sold. It's also worth pointing out that the probability of selling to a new prospect is between 5% and 20%, while the probability of selling to an existing customer is a whopping 60-70%[13].

63. Train, Train, Train Then Train Some More

Your staff should know:

a. Everything about the flower
b. Everything about the industry
c. Everything about customer service
d. Everything about personal selling

I have been in some dives of dispensaries but they had great, well-informed budtenders so I kept going back.

64. A Strip Joint or a Professional Cannabis Store

[13] http://www.salesradar.io/upselling-increases-sales-revenue/, by salesradario

Many cannabis stores make you want to look for the dancer's pole when you walk in. There is nothing wrong with tats, nose rings and bare midriffs. But look at the demographics of your customers. You will find that they are more sophisticated than you think and may enjoy a little more of a professional environment. The days of the headshops are gone.

65. Collect Happy Customer Testimonials

Don't keep it a secret if you have happy customers. You probably have customers that are raving fans of your store. Get their testimonies in writing and on video. People love to love what other people love. Put their videos on your website and in your emails. It is easier to have other people brag about you.

66. Home Parties

Remember the Tupperware ® parties of the 70's. A new twist on that is the private cannabis parties of the 2020's. It is a simple process on the surface. Get a list of customers and customer prospects. Send them an invitation. Supply some munchies and supply the best cannabis you can find. A private party is great for getting dispensaries to carry your product and reward your best customers.

There is a company in Massachusetts, Eat Sacrilicious that focuses on creating cannabis fine dining experiences. Their business model charges guests $225 that includes the meal, a cocktail reception, and membership to Eat Sacrilicous[14]. They are not just selling cannabis; they are selling an experience and offering the cannabis as a gift.

Check with your attorney, but as of this writing, you do not need a cannabis event license in California for any cannabis event that is private[15]. In California, your event is not private if you are doing any of these things:

1. Advertising the event to the public (i.e. no strict "invite only" policy or anyone can learn about the event online using a quick Google search)
2. Charging cover, selling tickets or accepting donations
3. Directly or indirectly selling cannabis goods
4. Holding the event on the premises of a licensed cannabis business

There still are not a lot of guidelines on hosting private cannabis parties in California. California's Alcohol Beverage Commission defines private party as follows:

5. The event is private, i.e. a bona fide guest list restricts access to invited guests ONLY.
6. There are no direct or indirect sales of cannabis, i.e. no ticket sales, donations, door charges, or weed costs – all cannabis must be complimentary and provided ONLY by the host.

---

[14] https://cannabiz.media/marijuana-dinner-parties-fine-dining-painting-parties-and-more/, Susan Gunelius | Jul 19, 2019 | Marijuana Industry
[15] https://www.thecannabist.co/2016/01/11/kendal-norris-cannabis-party-marijuana-mason-jar/46320/, By Ricardo Baca, The Cannabist Staff

7. The event venue does not require a BCC license or permit, i.e., the venue is not an establishment that regularly sells cannabis such as a dispensary or distributor.

67. Request Your Product Where it is Not Carried

Send staff members into stores in your target market area and ask for your brands. I like the brand Just Cannabis. They have a crumble called “Sugar” that is awesome. I went into my local dispensary and asked for it a couple of times and this on-the-ball dispensary called a few weeks later to tell me they now had it in stock.

Online Marketing

68. Answer Questions on Forums and Answer Sites

Help people with free advice on topics related to your products and services. You will gain their trust and will look more professional.

69. List Your Business in Local Business Directories

Google My Business from Google and Bing Places for Google from Bing are absolutely free for local businesses, while Yahoo Local works from Yahoo is a paid service allowing you to list your business in 50 directories (Yahoo Local, Yelp, White Pages, Bing,

MapQuest, etc.). Once you're listed, start taking advantage of local search results, and don't forget to ask your customers to leave reviews on your page.

70. Post Your Company Offers on Coupon & Deal Sites

People love special offers and discounts. Getting a great product at an excellent price is what everybody wants.

71. Create Infographics for Your Website

People love these small but highly descriptive graphical information displays. They can be used to drive links to your website and drive traffic.

72. Add Schema.org Markup to Your Website Key Data

Google can show much more than your website URL in search results. Reviews, ratings, exact address - all of it can show up in search engine results if your website HTML is marked properly. More data in search results = more clicks and traffic.

73. Do Guest Blogging

Guest blogging is a great white-hat SEO method that helps you get links and traffic. Being in the cannabis industry, people want our opinions and views. You give away quality content and get exposure in return. Quality backlinks coming to your website is a free bonus!

74. Comment on Other Blogs

Meaningful comments on other websites will get you traffic, free links, and new friends. Just remember - be meaningful and relevant. And yes - websites must be in the same industry/serving the same audience.

75. Claim Your Online Business Listings

There are hundreds of websites out there that contain your business information. Claim your business online and enjoy better rankings in Google, greater visibility, and more traffic.

76. Keep Your Website Fresh

Your customers should be coming to your website even when they are not buying some cannabis. There should be current news, white papers, tips, tricks and tools. Much like how you clean your dab rig.

77. Cannabis Friendly Ad Networks

There are ad networks that accept and even encourage cannabis advertising. These unique digital advertising platforms use display ads. An example of a cannabis friendly ad network is Traffic Roots. It targets niche audiences interested in music, yoga, sports, cannabis and other hip lifestyles. Include these cannabis friendly private networks and websites in your marketing plans. These networks are "native advertising" outlets. This describes any situation where branded messages fit seamlessly within their surrounding online environment, engaging audiences rather than disrupting the user experience.[16] A few other cannabis ad friendly networks are Taboola, Outbrain, and Mantis.84.

78. Join Local Chat Rooms

There are chat rooms about lifestyles, cannabis, mindfulness, entertainment, basically any subject you can think of. Don't just think about cannabis chat rooms. Think about lifestyle chatrooms.

79. Free Stuff

Offer free stuff on the website. White papers, user guides, current news, and entertainment digital books. I emphasize digital free stuff because it is easy to deliver. Don't offer free junk. Make your free stuff valuable. Make your site a destination website. If people just come to your site when they want to order product, they will only come to your website when they want to

[16] https://www.coladigital.ca/advertising-marijuana-products-native-ads/, Vee Popat

order product. If your customers want to hang out at your website, they will buy more.

80. Organic Search

Cannabis companies cannot advertise on Instagram, Facebook or Google, but you can still focus on organic reach. You can post "scholarly" articles on the subject of cannabis on almost any social media website. The more we educate society, the more people will understand the benefits of cannabis. Post often and on a consistent schedule. Watch your hash tags and keep them current. Educate, don't sell. Post frequent third-party articles about the healing powers of cannabis. Comment on other people's postings. Stay away from the pot-head type articles. These are not effective, and they hurt the industry. It may sound rather obvious, but they can't find you in searches if you aren't there.

81. User Generated Content

Get your website visitors to generate content for you. How about some free advertising this year? You can get that with user-generated content (UGC). Thanks to the advent of social media, other people can advertise for you in a way that does not even look like advertising. They can promote your brand to their friends and associates. When someone else brags about you, it's less tacky. One of the best ways to get the ball rolling on UGC is to ask people to post a picture of themselves with your product on social media using a specific hashtag. If you're marketing a service, ask them to tweet about how your service helped them, also using a specific hashtag. Be sure to share the best entries on your own social media timelines.

82. Video, Video, Video

Online video ads blow non-video ads out of the water. 3M, the company that makes the Post-it Notes says that visuals are processed 60,000 more times faster than text[17] People remember 80% of what they see and only about 20% of what they read.[18] Slick videos are not always the best videos. People want real, not slick. I have a friend that produced an infomercial for a curtain steam iron. It did not do very well on test, so he took it off the air for reediting. He had one scene he wanted to include but unfortunately in that scene, the demonstrator dropped the iron. The little imperfection, once added back into the infomercial, doubled the response rate and sales.

83. Advertise on Craigslist

Cannabis is openly advertised on Craigslist. At this moment there seems to be a sprinkling of cannabis shops, several seed offerings, tons of accessories and some shops for sale in the Los Angeles area Craigslist. This publication is always changing, but

---

[17] https://www.fastcompany.com/3035856/why-were-more-likely-to-remember-content-with-images-and-video-infogr
[18] https://www.pixelo.net/visuals-vs-text-content-format-better/

it is worth checking out. Type in the words “weed,” or “cannabis” and you get no results. Type in the word “bong” you will get lots of results. Use your head.

84. Online Cannabis Platforms

There are several online cannabis selling platforms. These companies do not “touch” the flower. They allow cannabis companies to reach the local cannabis markets in a deeper and broader way. These platforms market heavily, and you can benefit from these huge advertising spends. It is basically a pay to play situation. If you want to have your dispensary and/or brands on these platforms it will cost you. And they are building their own cannabis growing, manufacturing and retail capabilities right alongside their customer dispensaries.

It is an odd dance that dispensaries and brands are doing with the cannabis platforms. The platforms see the money and the wisdom in vertically integrating and eating their client dispensary lunches, competing with them, taking their businesses. And dispensaries are moving more into deliveries and building robust websites to compete with the platforms. The most popular cannabis platforms are:

1. Eaze
2. Greerush
3. Jane Technologies
4. Leaflink

5. Potvalet
6. Cannabase
7. Dutchie

It can make sense to pay the fees and advertise on some of these platforms but set up your accounting so that you can track the profitability of this revenue stream. If you are a brand marketer, it may make sense to use these platforms to get your brands out into dispensaries and into the hands of consumers. The bigger and more popular these platforms grow, the bigger and more popular they will be to your customer and they will be more formidable competitors.

85. Google Local and City Search

Get your business' address included on Google Local and CitySearch. It's free.

86. Programmatic Ad Buying, Not Google AdWords or Facebook Ads

Most online ad networks, including Google and Facebook, do not allow ads from marijuana-related businesses. That means you can't use the two biggest ad networks or many other smaller ad networks to get your ads in front of your target audience as they surf the web. So what do you do? Take your business elsewhere. There are several opportunities to display your ads to your target audience using programmatic ad buying. In simplest terms, with programmatic advertising, you use software (or pay someone to use the software for you) to place bids, display your ads on applicable websites, and optimize their performance. Try Adistry and Mantis which are both marijuana-friendly. https://cannabiz.media/5-proven-marijuana-marketing-and-advertising-ideas-that-work/

87. Brand Ambassadors

Social media is also about encouraging other people, brand ambassadors, to publish and share content about your brand and business (i.e., pulling content about your brand from other people). You can recruit brand ambassadors among your most loyal customers or hire brand ambassadors who are already influential with your target audience online (i.e., national and global celebrities or “online” celebrities) to create user-generated content about your brand. In addition, make it easier for all your customers to publish user-generated content related to your brand and business. Every dispensary uses brand ambassadors, but you can have your current customers be your brand ambassadors.

88. Tweet, Tweet, Tweet

Rather than investing in ads, focus on publishing useful content. Did you know that tweets from Twitter often rank higher than web pages in some Google searches? By publishing useful tweets, you might see one of your tweets at the top of a search results page where it could get significant exposure. According to Alfred Ng of CNET, this is a marketing tactic that has worked well for Jardin Premium Cannabis Dispensary in Las Vegas, Nevada.

89. Host Photo Contests Online

These contests are great in a lot of ways since they are easy to join. It also helps you, as the sponsor, to get user-generated content. You can reuse these and put them somewhere else to promote your business.

You can also host caption contests alongside these. You can post a photo and ask your audience to give their best caption for it. This can give you some good laughs while promoting organic engagement.

Personal marketing

90. People Listen to Hairdressers

Pay a hairdresser to talk to their clients about your awesome shop or kickass brand while in their chair. Make sure they have a stack of your first-time visitor card at their station.

91. Build a Referral Network

Referrals and word of mouth are the most powerful advertising, so build relationships with professionals and other businesses you would happily refer your customers to and who can send referrals your way, as well.

92. Create Customer Case Studies

Ask your happy customers to share their experience of using your product or service. These stories add credibility to your company and help you get more customers. Post them on your website.

93. Offer Free Consultations

Free consultations are a great way to showcase your expertise and get more clients.

94. Send Handwritten Holiday, Birthday, or Thank You Cards

Send these to past and current clients, valued partners, vendors in your referral network, connections who have helped you--everyone you can think of. This is a low-cost and unique marketing idea for small business, but many entrepreneurs have reported its effectiveness. If you are trying to set up one of your cannabis brands on a delivery platform or you are trying to get a dispensary to carry your brand, rise above the clutter and send the decision maker and his assistant (never forget the assistant) a hand written note. It is so rare to see handwritten notes. Make it a practice to send out a few handwritten notes every day.

95. Become a Guest Speaker

Register with a speaker's bureau. Get paid to promote your cannabis product.

Right after cannabis was legalized in California, I had my annual physical. While making small talk with my doctor, she asked about what project I was working on now. I told her I was an executive with a local fully integrated cannabis company. She asked me if I would come to speak to her physician's group and a group of her patients. Of course, I said yes. I get the publicity of the presentation by the medical group who will announce it to the hospital where they practice, and in the medical group's patient newsletter.

96. Put a Few Billboards on the Streets

https://dashtwo.com/blog/marijuana-billboard-examples/

The price of billboards can range from a couple thousand dollars to over ten thousand each per month. They are expensive, incredibly hard to track and they are effective.

Research

97. Know Your Competitor Brands as Well as Your Own

You should be watching your client from afar and up close. You should be doing this every week:

1. Visit competing company websites
2. Visit competing company stores
3. Hire a clipping service to clip all articles about your competitors
4. Observe the demographics of the customers you see enter their stores
5. Do a survey of the products that appear to be selling on your competitor sites. If the product keeps appearing in competitor ads, it is probably a good product to study
6. Observe competitor ads on billboards and in magazines
7. Do name searches online to see where, how, and why your competition is being talked about in the press
8. Observe their clientele
9. Watch their ads, specials, discounts, upsells and freebies
10. Periodically make a few purchases at their dispensary and observe their entire sales cycle

Joint Venturing

98. Sponsor a Yoga Weekend

https://studybreaks.com/culture/cannabis-yoga/

Yoga and cannabis just go together. Maybe buy some yoga mats with your logo on them for a local yoga studio. Of course, the yoga studio should advertise in your store. The demographics of people who practice yoga and who are cannabis users are pretty similar. People practice yoga for the following benefits:

1. Calm the mind
2. Relieve effects of stress
3. Enhance the mind-body connection

Cannabis users consume cannabis for the same reasons. Cannabis and yoga go together.

99. Sponsor a Mindfulness Weekend

The same benefits of yoga. A cannabis/ mindfulness weekend retreat could be a low cost event. Maybe make it for a day instead of a weekend.

100. Supply Drink Coasters to Local Bars

Supply beverage coasters with your logo to all the local drinking establishments. Katz40 (katzamericas.com) sells coasters that can be scented with that marijuana smell we all love. There are a lot of other partnership possibilities

101. Partner with Wedding Planners

Partner with wedding planners to supply cannabis products at weddings, bachelor and bachelorette parties etc. Nowadays, divorce parties are pretty hot.

https://www.cbs58.com/news/couples-are-getting-married-and-hiring- budtenders-to-serve-marijuana

At a Cannabis Wedding Expo in Boston, couples could visit over 30 booths featuring marijuana-themed services. The Expo featured everything from flowers to chocolate fountains infused with CBD to marijuana drinks perfect for a wedding toast.

Wedding planner Madlyne Kelly is the co-owner of Irie Weddings & Events. Most of her clients do not want a cannabis-themed wedding but they want cannabis available at their wedding for their guests to enjoy in a safe manner. "Budtenders" are the specialty at Irie Wedding & Events. Insured experts serve joints and other products to guests. Kelly says they walk guests through "smelling the different strains to see which one is going to be the best for them." The average cannabis bar from Irie Weddings & Events costs $750 dollars for a wedding with 100 people. That price does not include the cannabis, which the couple must buy themselves[19].

---

[19] By: CBS News, Posted: Nov 18, 2019 1:42 PM CDT

Conclusion

I kept 100 Smokin' Hot Cannabis Marketing short. You are busy. Go out and make some people happy and sell some cannabis. The choice is pretty simple – Market or go out of business.

What Industry Leaders are Saying about 100 Smokin' Hot Cannabis Marketing Hacks:

Eduardo Sliva, Vice President for Foottraffik

Marketing is often an afterthought for most entrepreneurs', the idea that "if you build it they will come" is not applicable in the Cannabis industry. "100 Smokin' Hot Cannabis Marketing Hacks" offers a quick and easy read, and a manuscript for the up and coming business entrepreneur looking to enter the cannabis industry.

Eduardo is considered a marketing visionary in the cannabis industry. As Vice President of Sales for Foottraffik, Eduardo Silva is passionate about dispensary marketing, connecting with cannabis businesses, and driving results. With nearly 20 years of experience in sales and marketing in the tech sector, Silva now helps clients increase their brand awareness and customer engagement through the use of digital marketing tools like SEO, PPC, and Mobile Display Ads. Foottraffik is a leading cannabis marketing software (SaaS) and online cannabis marketing agency based in San Francisco, CA.

Derrick Kravitz, CEO, Green Umbrella, Inc.

"100 Smokin' Hot Cannabis Marketing Hacks" identifies and explains how to incorporate and implement effective marketing techniques to survive AND THRIVE in the volatile cannabis industry. There are many tools and strategies that can be used to reach your target audience, this book teaches you "100" practical methods. Any young startup and/or emerging cannabis brand can benefit by incorporating these marketing techniques to maximize brand exposure - even if you have to work with a minimal marketing budget."

Derrick, CEO of Green Umbrella, Inc., and Extract Harmony is considered a visionary in the legal cannabis and CBD industries. Derrick is well known in the industry for his management skills and his cannabis manufacturing skills. He co-developed the popular brand, *Just Cannabis,* a leading brand of flower and further processed cannabis products. He also developed the successful line of Extract Harmony cannabis products.

Green Umbrella is the parent company of several California licensed cannabis operations. They currently house multiple cannabis brands including the Extract Harmony product line consisting of premium health and wellness cannabis products. Extract Harmony specializes in producing cannabis extracts, topicals, tinctures, inhalables, and gourmet edibles.

Tudor Marginean, Cannabis Marketing Consultant

"Whether you are a cannabis veteran looking to get into the licensed game, with lots of wisdom and knowledge acquired during years of Cannabis practice and 'street wars' or simply a newcomer or an investor looking to get into that same game and make a buck out of the greenrush,"100 Smokin' Hot Cannabis Marketing Hacks" has you fully covered! It's instructional, it's user-friendly, and most importantly it's full of smart and fun Marketing Hacks to help you take your cannabis business to the next level. So if you're looking for tested and trusted Marketing Hacks to launch or promote your cannabis business or brand,

search no further! This is probably that ONE book you'll need. It certainly helped me!"

Tudor Marginean is a leading food marketing and branding consultant based in Los Angeles. After 20+ years of experience, he took his passion for cannabis a whole level up when he decided to join the industry in 2018, right about the time California fully legalized the cannabis industry. He is well respected in the cannabis industry, working with and advising several cannabis growers and manufacturers on sales, distribution and brand marketing, with always an eye out for the new infused edible brands out there.

Oliver Summers, the Duke of Pico, Director of Retail and Regulatory, The Godfather of Southern California cannabis, big shot executive (Director of Retail and Regulatory) at one of the fastest growing fully integrated cannabis companies in California.

"As an over 30 year Cannabis industry veteran, I have seen the marketing change dramatically. While once you could only hope for a specific cannabis related event like the High Times Cup. Today there are cannabis products being advertised at major sporting events, and are regarded just as normal as lcohol. "100 Smokin' Cannabis Marketing Hacks" helps navigate the cannabis landscape, understand the consumer, and help propel a brand to prominence in a crowded industry.

Oliver Summers is a Los Angeles Medical Cannabis advocate/Dispensary operator since 2005. He is also an experienced grower of boutique cannabis strains. Board member of the Southern California Coalition (SCC). Original board member and moderator of the Greater Los Angeles Collective Alliance (GLACA); Member of Americans For Safe Access (ASA), Marijuana Policy Project (MPP), and former member of UFCW Local 770. Oliver earned the title of "Duke of Pico" from being one of the most knowledgeable purveyors of cannabis on the Los Angeles marijuana scene. In addition to being one of the smartest pot guys around he is an astute businessman. He is now the Director of Retail and Compliance reporting directly to the CEO of one of the most successful fully integrated cannabis companies in California.

Other Books by Darrell Griffin

Believers Cannabis Guide (Summer 2021)

Another 100 Smokin' Hot Cannabis Marketing Hacks – Vol 2 (Winter 2021)

More Smokin' Hot cannabis Marketing Hacks – Vol 3 (Spring 2022)

Still More Smokin' Hot Cannabis Marketing Hacks – Vol 4 (Summer 2022)

Cannabis Accounting and Bookkeeping – (January 2022)

Cannabis KPI's and Analysis – (Winter 2022)

Last Journey – (Summer 2010, Edition 2, 2022) The true story of Darrell's embed with his son's combat unit in Baghdad during the "Surge."

Business With A Purpose – (2012, new edition Summer 2022) a 600 page guide for people wanting to start, manage, grow and protect a business. A "nuts-and-bolts" guide for believers starting a new business

Christian Informercial Guide – Direct response television techniques for believers

Trouble Bound (Spring 2022) – The true store of a teenager wrongly tried as an adult and sentenced to live in prison without parole.

God Think (Fall 2021) – Enhancing your God given creative thinking skills

About the Author

Darrell Griffin, CPA/MBA, grew up around the cannabis industry. His father, David Ross Griffin, was a member of an outlaw biker gang and cannabis was always around the house. Darrell was the Chief Financial and Operational Officer for one of the fastest growing, fully integrated cannabis companies in California. He has been a consultant to a number of leading cannabis companies in the areas of accounting, operations, marketing, and financing. He lives in the Los Angeles area with his wife, Kim, a controller for a major wine importing and distribution company, his son Jordan, his mother-in-law, sister-in-law, and their German Shepherd, Penny, and little terrier, Lucky. He is the author of *Last Journey*, *Business with a Purpose, Believers*

Cannabis Guide (Spring 2021). Darrell is a member of the Cannabis Marketing Association and Co-Founder of the Cannabis Business Group.

Made in the USA
Las Vegas, NV
22 October 2021